8085
CAR

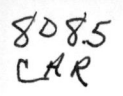

Speaking in Church Made Simple

A Step-by-Step Guide

C. Mitchell Carnell, Jr.

BETTY WILSON LIBRARY
Epworth UMC
3002 Hope Valley Road
Durham, NC 27707

BROADMAN PRESS
Nashville, Tennessee

© Copyright 1985 • Broadman Press
All Rights Reserved
4234-31
ISBN: 0-8054-3431-3

Dewey Decimal Classification Number: 808.5
Subject Headings: PUBLIC SPEAKING
Library of Congress Catalog Number: 84-27447

Printed in the United States of America

Library of Congress Cataloging in Publication Data

Carnell, C. Mitchell.
  Speaking in church made simple.

  1. Public speaking—Religious aspects—Christianity.
I. Title.
PN4121.C27 1985   808.5′1   84-27447
ISBN 0-8054-3431-3 (pbk.)

To my Mother and Father

If you cannot preach like Peter, if you cannot pray like Paul,
You can tell the love of Jesus and say He died for all.

—"Balm in Gilead"
Traditional Black Spiritual

Contents

Acknowledgements 7
Preface 9
1. The Enemy 13
2. Establishing the Battle Plan 17
3. Preparing for the Battle 21
4. Choosing a Topic 27
5. Planning the Speech 31
6. Practice! Practice! Practice! 35
7. Taking Care of Details and of Yourself 39
8. The Battle Is Joined 43
9. Pay Attention to Your Voice 47
10. Speeches of Introduction 55
Appendix 59
References 64

Acknowledgments

How do you acknowledge a lifetime of support, encouragement, inspiration, and persistence? My early training as a speaker began at Northside Baptist Church in Woodruff, South Carolina, through all of its organizations, and carried me from a preschool Sunbeam to an adult guest speaker.

I owe much to Sam Brissie who was superintendent of schools in Woodruff, who also taught a speech course. He has remained a counselor and friend. Sara Lowrey, long-time professor of speech at Furman University, was an inspiration beyond measure. She challenged us on a daily basis to strive for excellence in everything we did. Dr. Ollie Bacus at the University of Alabama and the late Dr. George Gunn at Louisiana State University continued the challenge.

Louise Carpenter of the Charleston Speech and Hearing Center has typed and retyped this manuscript until she can recite chapter and verse.

My Sunday School class at First Baptist Church,

Charleston, my graduate classes, and the people who have been enrolled in my workshops and seminars are due a special thank-you for they have been constantly exposed to all of the techniques and procedures mentioned here.

My family continues to offer encouragement for my efforts to help people find their voices to express their deepest thoughts and feelings.

For all of these expressions of love and encouragement I am grateful.

C. MITCHELL CARNELL, JR.
CHARLESTON, SOUTH CAROLINA

Preface

This book is for the person who is thwarted at every turn by one of mankind's most ancient enemies—stage fright, or literally speech fright. If speech fright is your problem, this book is for you.

There is no simple solution to the problem, but there is a program that, when followed step by step, will help *you* overcome *your* problem. Only you can take action to overcome the problem. The best time to begin is now.

This book has several objectives, but all of them are intended to help you attain your goal as a public speaker and thus release your potential for greater Christian service.

The objectives of this book are:

To help the Christian become a more effective communicator.
To help the Christian overcome stage fright.
To help the Christian become a more effective public speaker.

To help the Christian become a more effective listener.

To help the Christian become a more effective witness.

To help the Christian develop his/her leadership potential.

To help the Christian become a more effective Christian.

Other attractions that vie for our attention use all of the skills available to make their point. They use the technology and tremendous talents of the advertising industry to package and sell their products. The Christian must also be prepared to meet the competition in the marketplace. If we are to be effective fishers of men we must be willing to speak up for Christ, at every appropriate opportunity, and we must learn how to make the most of each opportunity—both public and private.

Several years ago, Larry Crisman, director of public relations for the South Carolina Baptist Convention, told a group of men gathered for a prayer breakfast, "Unless Southern Baptists and other Christians are creative, clever, and willing to wage war for the attention of modern man, they face an impossible task in communicating the gospel message.

"To be sure," he continued, "we still have the greatest story ever told, but unless we tell it in more meaningful and creative ways, we will lose the most important battle ever waged. Never in the history of

Preface

Christianity has the church faced a greater challenge."

If you are determined to overcome your fear of speaking in public and to become a more involved Christian, read on.

1
The Enemy

Stage fright—that cold, clammy feeling, dry mouth, trembling voice, shortening of breath, and pounding heart that attacks instantly when someone mentions speaking in public—has been known and feared for centuries.

Moses was well-acquainted with this disorder. According to Exodus 4:10 he had such a severe case of stage fright that he begged God to find someone else for His mission. Some authorities claim that Moses was a stutterer while others believe he suffered from a mild neurological disorder known as cluttering.

God finally grew so impatient with Moses' whimpering that He gave Moses a magic rod to hold onto and allowed Aaron, Moses' brother, to speak for Moses. This probably was the beginning of the modern field of speech pathology. Speakers are still holding onto things to comfort themselves—podiums, pencils, and loose change or keys. Many try to find someone to speak for them.

My father understands stage fright. In fact, he and Moses could share a great many experiences. Once when he was called on for a brief talk while visiting an out-of-town meeting of his lodge, he managed enough courage to mumble, "I always bring along a friend to do my talking for me." He followed Moses' example. Some might call this the Mosaic tradition.

Moses and my father are not alone. When 2,543 Americans were asked to rank a list of fears, 40.6 percent listed speaking before a group in first place. Fear of heights was a distant second at 32 percent. A fear of insects and bugs ranked third at 22.1 percent and fear of financial problems ranked fourth.

More women (46 percent) have this fear than men (36 percent). More people living in the Southern United States have this fear than people living in other parts of the country.

Many potentially good leaders are lost to churches and other groups on account of this one dreaded afflication—stage fright or speech fright.

Norman Vincent Peale, the famed minister of Marble Collegiate Church in New York and renowned author and speaker, was almost lost to the world because of stage fright. According to Peale, his first public appearance was almost a disaster. If a little girl seated in the front row had not laughed at his shaking knees and made him angry, he would not have continued.

In an interview with Eugene White in 1966, Peale

said in describing his first public speech, "When I stood up, I became literally stiff with fear. I couldn't get the first word out. In the embarrassed silence, a little girl in the front row giggled to her mother, 'Gosh, look at his knees shake.' That made me so angry that I found my voice and gave a spirited speech."

Linda Kelsey, who portrayed Billie Newman on the award-winning "Lou Grant" television show, has been nominated for four Emmys and two Golden Globe Awards. At age thirty-six she is very involved with her career.

With all of Linda's success she says, "People assume that because I am an actress, I can do anything. It's not true. I still have difficulty making speeches. They terrify me!"

Sally Ride, America's first woman astronaut, says that the toughest part of her job is the knife-and-fork circuit.

Since her history-making journey into space Mrs. Ride has averaged one speech a day traveling across this country and Europe.

Following her speech to the American Bar Association in Atlanta on August 1, 1983, a woman asked, "Were you ever afraid?"

"I was a lot more scared getting up to give this speech," she replied.

All good speakers confess that they are never completely free of stage fright. There is always some degree of uneasiness.

Now in his mid-sixties, Keenan Wynn is perhaps the most widely known character actor in the United States today. In a conversation with me this actor with more than 300 films to his credit said, "I've never gotten over stage fright. My first scene in any production is always a mess, and I have to film it over. After the first scene, I settle down and everything is fine."

The challenge is not how to rid yourself completely of stage fright but how to bring it under control. You want stage fright to work for you and not against you. How do you accomplish this?

2
Establishing the Battle Plan

If you are determined to do battle with stage fright and to master the art/science of public speaking, you need a battle plan. All good generals know that the best defense is a good offense.

University of Maryland football coach, Bobby Ross, relates that one of the problems in playing the Tigers of Louisiana State University at Baton Rouge, is the anxiety that is built up when the opposing team rushes onto the field only to be met by the ferocious growling of the LSU mascot, Mike the Tiger, and the tremendous noise made by eighty thousand fans screaming, "Tiger bait! Tiger bait! Tiger bait!" According to Ross, it takes the opposing team several minutes to recover from this anxiety, and by that time the score is fourteen to nothing. Ross says the opposing team must prepare for this. The team must be ready and must have its own plan. The same is true in the battle with stage fright. You must be ready and you must have your own plan.

The first step is for you to determine the conditions for the battle. You develop the strategy. Part of the problem is that we allow fear to build up over every situation. We become so fearful that we will be called upon to speak that we work ourselves into a panic. Some people even avoid situations in which they might be called on to talk. You can short-circuit this reaction. The secret is for you to choose the time and the conditions.

Be Selective

Now that you have resolved to conquer stage fright, make the circumstances as favorable to yourself as possible. Look around for your opportunity to begin. You choose it. Do not allow someone else to stampede you before you are ready. You are in command.

Decide that you will read the opening Scripture in Sunday School or that you will take the lead in the responsive reading, that you will give the devotion, or offer the closing prayer in midweek prayer service.

You may decide to take an active role in one of the women's or men's organizations. You may have a strong desire to present your convictions on tithing during the stewardship campaign. You may want to share a book of great interest with a study group. There are literally dozens of opportunities during any week at even the smallest church.

Consult your calendar. Choose a date for the battle. Be realistic. Don't choose a date so near that you will not be ready or so far in the future that you will worry yourself into a frenzy. Two or three weeks in the future should be ample time, but you must make that decision.

Make a commitment. It is not enough to tell yourself that you will do this. You must tell someone else. Commit your decision to writing. Call the leader of the group and discuss what you want to do and when. Agree on the date. The leader will help you decide on what to do and when to do it. He is not only interested in you as a person but also because church leaders are always eager to develop new talent.

If you had rather make your first appearance before a group other than one in which you are a member, talk to the director of religious education. She will help you select an appropriate group.

Some people find it easier at first to talk to children, perhaps by reading a Bible story or telling a story to them. Some added security is usually present since it is desirable to sit while reading or telling a story to young children.

Reading the Bible passage from a modern translation is often a good place to begin. A modern translation is recommended only because of the timely vocabulary and the more familiar sentence structure. There are also excellent Bible story books available. Start with something quite easy.

Spend some time browsing in your church library or in a religious book store. You will be amazed at the variety of materials available to you.

You have now (1) decided to conquer speech fright, (2) decided on a plan, (3) made a commitment to yourself and someone else, and (4) selected a date for a public appearance.

Possible First Choices

Read the Scripture aloud
Read a prepared devotional aloud
Paraphrase a prepared devotional
Present an original devotional
Read a prepared prayer
Pray an original prayer
Read a Bible story aloud
Narrate a Bible story using pictures or filmstrip
Tell a Bible story from memory
Read someone else's testimony
Read your own testimony
Give your own testimony from notes
Give your own testimony without notes
Read the announcements
Introduce a speaker
Give a committee report

3
Preparing for the Battle

Prepare! The most important weapon against stage fright is *thorough preparation.*

Obtain the materials you plan to use. If you are developing the material yourself, then you should start to prepare it. If you are using someone else's material, obtain it and read through it. For example, if you are using a devotional that has been published, you have two ways to proceed. You can read it aloud word-for-word to the group or you can do your own summary. Decide which approach you will use.

For the first time let's suppose that you decide to read aloud from the Bible to the group. Select the passage as soon as possible. When you have made your choice, read the passage through several times.

Use a tape recorder as you read. A small cassette-type player is the easiest to use and most often available. If you do not own one, you can borrow one from your church's media center or from a friend. Learn to use it correctly. Make friends with it. Play with it.

Get comfortable with it. Listen to yourself. Make whatever changes you think are necessary and practice again.

Practice talking or reading into the tape recorder while standing and looking into a mirror. This will help you remember to keep a pleasant look on your face. Smile! Stand straight. A good appearance is important.

Reading aloud is truly an art. Can you recall hearing the Bible read well? What effect did that have on you? Think of the service you could render to others by learning the art of reading well. You can do it.

The secret of effective oral reading of the Bible is preparation. Choose a selection from a translation which you like and become familiar with it. For pure beauty of words and phrase, the King James version is the overwhelming favorite. However, it is one of the most difficult to read aloud.

My preference is for *The New Testament in Modern English,* a translation by J. B. Phillips; however, I often use the *Living Bible* or *Good News for Modern Man.* The translation or version you use is simply a matter of personal preference unless you are a member of a denomination or group that frowns on the use of modern translations. If there is any doubt about which version to use, use the King James version. Never deliberately offend someone. You want them to listen.

Before you read orally from the Bible to a group,

practice reading the selection silently several times. Think about what you are reading. Ask yourself these questions. Who is speaking? Who is being spoken to? What is the speaker's mood, the listener's mood? What are the circumstances surrounding the passage? Who is present?

Close the Bible and think about the passage. Tell it in your own words. Now read it aloud. Read it aloud again. Repeat this exercise several times.

Read the passage into the tape recorder. Play it back and listen carefully. How do you sound? Did you stumble over any words? Are there any words in the passage that you are uncertain about in terms of their pronunciation or meaning? Write each difficult word on a three-by-five-inch index card.

Look up each troublesome word in a modern dictionary or a Bible dictionary. Write the meaning and the pronunciation of each word on the appropriate index card. Practice saying these words. Use each one in a sentence. Speak them into the tape recorder. Play the tape. Do you pronounce them easily?

If you will be standing when you read to the group, practice reading aloud while standing. Practice in front of a full-length mirror with the tape recorder turned on.

Look up from the printed script. Look at yourself in the mirror as if you were the audience. Smile at yourself.

Arrange to read the passage for your family. Ask them to listen for interest, content, and smoothness.

Ask them to note whether or not you maintain a pleasant expression on your face and whether or not you establish and maintain eye contact. Ask them if they understand the passage.

Practice reading into the tape recorder again. Listen to your recording. Repeat this at least twice each day until the day of your public appearance. Once in the morning and again in the evening is better than doing all of your rehearsing at one time. At last, you are ready.

All of these steps also apply if you are reading anything other than the Bible. Bible stories, prepared devotionals, short essays, and exerpts from great literature all lend themselves to this procedure.

The secret is to be so familiar with what you are reading that you can look up from it frequently. You should be able to look at your listener and still locate your place on the page without any difficulty.

You may want to retype the passage double- or triple-spaced onto regular typing paper using only one side of the paper. This will permit you to underline any words for specific attention or to make notes for guidance. Use short lines so that you can scan them easily. You may want to use a typewriter with large type such as those used to make name tags at conventions, or you could type everything in capital letters.

If you have a visual problem or a physical disability that would prevent you from using printed materials to prepare, you may obtain recordings of the Bible from the Talking Book Division of the Library of Congress. Your local librarian can assist you in making the necessary arrangements. There are also commercially produced recordings of the Bible. Your denominational bookstore will be able to assist you in this.

The J. B. Phillips translation of the New Testament mentioned earlier comes in a large print edition. So does *Open Windows,* a quarterly book of devotions published by the Sunday School Board of the Southern Baptist Convention. Check with the publishing division of your denomination.

4
Choosing a Topic

You have decided to make a short talk to the opening assembly for the adult Sunday School department, but you have not been given a topic. You must select your own subject. What do you do?

Before you panic, analyze the situation. What do you know about it?

You know that your audience will be made up of adult men and women. You know the date and you know the time limit—ten minutes. Find your Sunday School quarterly and look through it. What is the theme of the lessons for the date you have chosen? What is the overall theme for the month or quarter? Do any of these hold a special interest for you? Could you develop a talk that would enhance your listeners' appreciation and understanding of the overall theme for the month or quarter? If you choose something related to the day's lesson, be courteous to the teachers by avoiding material they may cover in class. Put yourself in the teacher's place.

Do you have some particular knowledge or experience in one of the subject areas? Have you read an article or book recently that deals with the subject?

Brouse through a book of daily devotionals such as *Open Windows, The Upper Room,* or *Daily Blessings.* Does anything here interest you? It is not necessary to stick with the current issues or just the articles. Sometimes the life of one of the writers will furnish the raw material for your talk. Glance through your church or denominational calendar. Are there special events that should be stressed that might otherwise go unnoticed? Has your minister touched on a topic recently that you would like to explore more fully? He would be flattered and could probably suggest additional references.

You are ready to decide. Do not teach the Sunday School lesson and do not settle for making announcements. Use the time wisely. Select a topic that interests you. Chances are if the topic interests you it will interest others as well. One of the most important causes for failure is lack of interest in the subject by either the speaker or the listener.

One Sunday morning my wife asked me, "What on earth were you doing singing the 'Itsy Bitsy Spider' in the shower this morning? I like it. I sing it with my kindergarten children, but what were *you* doing?"

"I was thinking about all the good philosophy it teaches," I said.

"The spider works and works to climb the water spout. He almost makes it and then is washed out. He tries again. The sun always comes out just as it does in our daily lives. The sun always comes out in the end. What a good subject for a talk this is," I continued.

At the funeral of the mother of a good friend, the choir, organist, and pianist participated in a beautiful arrangement of children's hymns. It was a moving experience because the mother had given fifty years of her life to teaching children in Sunday School. Her fifty years of devotion were beautifully wrapped up in hymns such as "Jesus Loves Me," and "Jesus Loves the Little Children of the World." What a thoughtful and wonderful tribute and what a marvelous topic for a devotional talk.

When I was a student at Mars Hill College in North Carolina, our minister told the story of a wealthy woman who paid a household worker by giving her old shoes. He built his sermon around the theme of giving God less than our best, or paying Him off with what we have left over. "God does not want our hand-me-downs," he said.

Several years ago I gave a devotional using our historic First Baptist Church in Charleston, South Carolina, as the theme. In it I asked the question, "Where do we place the emphasis—*First, Baptist,* or *Church,* and where does God place the emphasis?

Do not overlook your favorite passage of Scripture as an excellent topic for your talk. Give the background. Why does it have special significance for you? How did it come to be your favorite? What do other Christians say about it?

While writing this book, I learned that my wife and my mother have in common a favorite verse of Scripture—"Let the words of my mouth and the meditation of my heart be acceptable in thy sight, O Lord, my strength and my redeemer" (Ps. 19:14).

Topics are all around you. You hear them on the radio, see them on television, read them in the newspaper, or discover them in conversations with friends. The difficulty is selecting. Talk about something you know.

At the 1982 Blue Ridge Christian Writer's Conference, Rev. Ken Barney, editor of *Live,* used the inspiration of an early morning walk through the woods in the crisp mountain air to fashion an effective devotional.

Once you have decided, do not discard the other possibilities. Write each topic you have chosen on a three-by-five-inch index card and file it for future use. Collect any additional information that you may have on the subject and file it for safekeeping with the topic card. Soon you will have collected more good topics for talks than you will be able to use.

You will find that you are surrounded by topics just waiting to be explored.

You have now (1) decided to make a ten-minute talk to the opening assembly of an adult Sunday School class, and (2) you have selected a topic. You are making progress toward your goal.

5
Planning the Speech

You have chosen your topic, and now you are ready to begin planning the speech. You have already accomplished much of the preparation in selecting the topic. Now, you want to support your choice. You want to share with us why the topic is important.

Think about the purpose of your talk. What do you want to accomplish? Do you want to entertain us? Probably not for your first speech since this is one of the most difficult speeches to make.

Do you want to inform or instruct us about some new discovery or procedure?

Do you want to convince or persuade us to take a specific course of action?

Do you want to inspire us to make some greater achievement? Write your purpose on a fresh five-by-eight inch index card.

The organization of a speech is very simple. Keep

in mind that a speech must have a beginning, a middle or body, and a conclusion.

Get a fresh stack of five-by-eight inch index cards. On the first card write the topic for your talk. Next write a trial sentence that represents the major emphasis of your talk. It will require several attempts before you are satisfied. This will become your opening sentence. This sentence along with some introductory remarks forms your introduction.

The introductory sentence is very important because it prepares your audience for what it is about to hear. It sets the stage. You will want to try several drafts before you decide on the one you will use. Do not become discouraged. Keep working at it. Make it as interesting as possible.

The Body

What are the major points you would like to cover in your talk? Write each one on a separate index card. Do you have any examples that you would like to use in your talk that are appropriate to any one of the points you have written? If so, write an example under the appropriate sentence. Are there any specific facts or references that you would like to note? If so, write this information in the appropriate spot. Check over what you have written. Have you included the information that caused you to choose this particular topic?

Arrange these cards in order from the most important to the least important. These points along with a few transition statements will form the body of your speech. Go through your cards once more. Are you happy with your arrangement? Are there any weak points? Remove those cards or find the information that will strengthen them. Remember two or three strong points are more desirable than five or six weak ones. People can easily forget six points, but one point clearly made can change lives.

The Conclusion

What thought would you like to leave with your audience? What do you want us to do? Do you want us to contribute money or engage in daily Bible reading, invite someone else to church, come to a picnic, be baptised, paint the youth center, pray more, or do you just want us to think about what you have said? Write your answer on one of your index cards. This is your conclusion.

This summary is your final opportunity to drive your point home.

The point must be clearly and concisely stated, and to do this it must be kept simple and straightforward.

Avoid words such as *lastly, finally,* and *in conclusion.* These are weak words and detract from your meaning. Consider the following conclusion:

We have fifty children in our neighborhood day care center who will get no toys for Christmas. There will be no Santa Claus for them unless you help.

We want each family to sign up to bring at least one toy for one of these boys or girls to the church office no later than December 10th.

Mrs. Davis and Mr. Johnson are seated at the table in the back of the room so that you can sign up as you leave.

Make certain that no little boy or girl goes without a toy for Christmas. It is up to you. They have no one else to turn to. Sign up for toys for tots.

You now have the skeleton and some of the meat for your speech.

6
Practice! Practice! Practice!

Preparation is the key to a good presentation. Nothing else matters nearly as much. You must make the time to practice.

Once you have your material prepared and you know what your purpose is, what your main points are, and what your conclusion is, you are ready to rehearse.

You will need your notes, your tape recorder, and an alarm clock that is easy to read.

Go to a quiet room where you will not be disturbed. If this is not possible, wait until the family has gone to work or to bed or has left the premises. You might need to get up early before anyone else to accomplish this.

Set the clock alarm for ten minutes. Now, read your notes aloud. Stop when the alarm sounds. How far did you get through your notes?

Note the time and read through the remainder of

your notes. How much longer was required? Now you know the extent of your problem.

Set the clock again for ten minutes. Switch on the tape recorder. Stand up and go through your talk. Stop when the alarm sounds. How far did you get this time?

If you had time left, that's great. Did you leave out any vital points or information? If not, you are all set.

If you ran out of time, where can you make cuts? Listen to your tape recording. Did you cover most of the points? Were you too wordy? Did you use too many examples? Did you allow the tape recorder to run while you were just thinking? Decide on what you can reasonably omit and remove those notes.

Rearrange your cards to reflect your changes. Set the alarm for ten minutes. Switch on the tape recorder. Read your notes aloud. Stop when the alarm sounds. How far did you get? Great!

Now you have your talk together. You can begin to practice in earnest. Continue to use the tape recorder and the clock.

Stand in front of a full-length mirror. If you do not have a full-length mirror, then a smaller one that extends to your waist is your next best choice. Turn on the tape recorder. Give your opening statement. Play back the recording. How did it sound? Were you pleased? How did you look? Did you remember to smile? Go through the opening statement again.

Now, give your closing statement. Remember this

Practice! Practice! Practice!

is the thought you want to leave with the audience. This is what you want them to remember. Hit it hard. Give it your best. Play back the recording. How did it sound? Were you convinced?

You are ready to rehearse again. Stand in front of the mirror. Turn on the tape recorder. This time go through your entire speech from start to finish. Play it back. How did it sound?

From now until the day of your presentation, rehearse at least twice each day. Remember that two short rehearsals are more effective than one long rehearsal. If you have family or friends around, ask them to listen to you once or twice. Don't ask them to listen to every rehearsal.

During idle moments take out your note cards and read them. Do not memorize. Become so familiar with them that you are not dependent on them. You want to be able to maintain good eye contact with your audience.

If you have followed these directions, you have done a good job. You will be ready for your presentation.

7
Taking Care of Details and of Yourself

Choose your clothing early. This is important for it will give you one less detail to worry about. If necessary, send your garment out to be cleaned at least one week before your talk. If you are planning to wear something new, be sure to put it on and practice at least once looking into the mirror. Check the garment carefully.

Soon after relocating to Charleston, I went to one of the most important receptions of my career wearing a new suit with the price tag still attached to the sleeve. It was fortunate that I was not speaking at that function or I would have been so unnerved that I probably would have walked out. If I had followed this system at that time I would not have been so embarassed. If you take care of these small details in advance, you can simply go to your closet and take out your preselected clothing. You have already made the decision as to what to wear. Do not consider last-minute changes.

There are several books on the market that deal with how to dress for different occasions. You may find one of these helpful; however, for most occasions simple business dress is appropriate. This could be a greater problem for women than for men. Always aim for simplicity and good taste.

If you need transportation, arrange for it in advance.

Later when you are an old pro at speechmaking you will need to be concerned about slides or overhead projectors, but not now.

Most people find it best to eat lightly before a speech or public appearance. This is something that you will learn to judge for yourself.

There are numerous occasions where food is served before a speech.—annual loyalty dinner, sweetheart banquet, deacon's banquet, special emphasis week, etc. It may be very simple such as a prayer breakfast or visitation luncheon. Even so, you may want to eat lightly and enjoy a full meal when it is all over. Alcohol and speechmaking do not mix. Neither does alcohol and effective listening. It will not relax you. It will only make you less alert and less in control.

Fatigue is a constant enemy. Be sure to get an adequate amount of sleep and rest. Do not burn the candle at both ends before you are scheduled to talk. You want to be as physically and mentally alert as possible.

Taking Care of Details and of Yourself

You have now (1) decided to overcome speech fright, (2) made a commitment, (3) obtained a date to speak, (4) selected a topic, (5) researched the topic, (6) planned the talk, (7) rehearsed the talk, (8) selected your clothing, and (9) arranged for transportation. You are ready.

8
The Battle Is Joined

The big day has arrived. It is time for you to make your presentation. You are prepared. The biggest part of the job is now behind you. You have done your homework.

Follow these simple step-by-step procedures to score a major victory for yourself.

Get dressed in plenty of time, but not too early.

Wear the clothes you selected in advance. Do not make last-minute changes. Of course, you can add a topcoat or a raincoat.

Read your notes through in a relaxed manner. Be certain that they are arranged in the proper order. Number them on the front if you have not already done so.

Rehearse your opening and closing statements.

Leave your home in time to get to the lecture room at least thirty minutes early.

Familiarize yourself with the arrangements of the

room. If people are not already seated in the audience, try the lectern and the microphone if available.

Take a seat on the front row of the audience, not on stage or behind a table.

Stay relaxed as you wait.

When the moment comes and you are introduced, take a deep breath and let it out slowly. Do this in an inconspicuous manner. As you stand press the tips of your fingers firmly against the seat of your chair. Again, slowly let the fingers relax. These exercises will help displace your tension.

Walk to the lectern in an unhurried but purposeful manner.

Face the audience and stand quietly. Wait a few seconds before you begin. Not only will this help you settle down, it will create a sense of expectation in the audience.

Begin.

Look at your audience. Establish eye contact with several people in different areas of the room. You have prepared well for this moment.

Talk with your audience—not at it. Share in a conversational manner your thoughts as you would with a friend. Just tell them the things you want them to know. Tell them the things that are important to you. Tell them why this topic is important to you.

Do not rush, but keep the pace lively.

When you have finished your talk, stay at the lectern for a few seconds. Look at your audience.

If there are any questions, take them one by one. Repeat the question for all to hear before you answer it.

Rephrase the question if it will help to clarify it. Answer the question in a loud, clear voice. Do not hedge.

If the questions require more information than you have, offer to obtain it. If it is a controversial or technical question, you may want to answer it or you may want to refer it to another person. If it is not appropriate for the occasion, do not hesitate to state that you would be happy to discuss the matter privately, but that it is not appropriate for this audience.

Never attempt to make your audience believe that you know the answer to a question when you do not. In these cases simply state in a straight forward, unapologectic manner, "I do not know the answer to your question."

Never put a questioner down or try to make the questioner feel uncomfortable.

Never ridicule a questioner.

When the question and answer period is over, thank the audience and take your seat.

Congratulations!

You have followed through on your commitment to become a public speaker. You are ready to find the next opportunity.

9
Pay Attention to Your Voice

Some people react with disbelief the first time they hear their voice played back on a tape recorder.

"Do I sound like that?" they ask in astonishment.

After being assured that indeed they do sound like that, most people are ready to pay some attention to their voices. Voices are just as individual as your fingerprints. They reflect the total personality of the speaker.

Most voices, even untrained ones, are more than adequate for speaking in public. With a little attention they will become even better.

Think of the most pleasant voice you have ever heard. Try to get a visual image of its owner. Focus on the image of that person speaking. Look at his or her face. Are they smiling? What are they wearing? Where are they standing? Is it morning, afternoon, or night? Try to hear the voice. What is it that you like so much about this voice? The sound is there in your auditory memory. Concentrate!

Does your voice have some of the same characteristics that you like so much about your favorite voice? What are they?

- Is it enthusiastic?
- Is the volume appropriate for the situation?
- Is it easily understood?
- Is the rhythm natural?
- Is the rate appropriate?

When you are rehearsing your presentation, try to remember this list and include as many of the favorable characteristics as possible. It will take time and practice.

Now that you have discovered your auditory memory, focus for a moment on the most unpleasant voice that you remember. Try to get a visual image as you did before. Who is speaking? What is the occasion? Is the speaker smiling? Where is the speaker? What time of day is it? Listen to the voice. What are its characteristics?

- Is it too loud or can you barely hear it?
- Is it harsh or metallic-sounding?
- Does it make you shudder because it sounds like fingernails scraping on a chalkboard?
- Is it too sluggish or lifeless?
- Is it nasal or does the person sound as if they have a mouthful of cotton?

What about the speaker's rate? Does she speak so

rapidly that you cannot understand or do you yawn waiting for the next word?

Does your voice have any of these characteristics? Make a list. These are the ones you want to eliminate.

Our voices give a loud, clear picture of our emotional status and of our physical well-being. When we feel confident, our voice will be strong, well-modulated, and appropriately paced. We will give off signals of strength and sincerity.

If we are nervous and unsure of ourselves, our voices will tremble, become nasal or strident, and we will speak more rapidly. Our voice can easily betray the strength or weakness of our position.

In its heyday, radio made extensive use of vocal characteristics to help establish the image of the character. There were no visual cues to help as there are today with television.

Remember the strong, unfaultering, commanding voice of the Lone Ranger or Perry Mason? There was never any doubt as to the rightness of their cause or the flawlessness of their character.

Remember the unmistakable goodness in the voice of Cinderella and the ugliness present in the voices of her wicked stepsisters? No one ever had to explain which was good and which was evil.

Mrs. Bufforfinton on Dagwood and Blondie reeked of wealth and "high society" in the way she oozed out each well-formed syllable. Even the sound of her car was used to complete the picture. It purred.

Much of Walter Cronkite's success is due to his strong, commanding voice. It engenders confidence. It says, "Walter is telling the truth."

Although there is only one Walter Cronkite, you will want your voice to give the same impression: "I am a trustworthy person. Follow me."

One of your best tools for improving the quality of your voice is your tape recorder. Become good friends with it. Record your conversations and your presentations. Listen to yourself. Block out the factual content on the tape and listen only to the way you sound.

Become a good listener to other voices. Listen for those things that please you and for those things that are displeasing. Make a list. What characteristics make that voice so pleasant to listen to? Most likely the speaker articulates each word clearly. He speaks at a moderate rate. You do not have to strain to hear what he says or cover your ears because you are being bombarded.

There are many opportunities to listen to good voices. Ten prominent personalities of stage, screen, radio, and television have been honored by the American Speech-Language and Hearing Association as having exemplary voices. The 1983 "best voice" awards included stage and screen stars Gregory Peck, the late Richard Burton, Julie Andrews, Sean Connery, Orson Wells, and James Earl Jones; radio commentator Paul Harvey; NBC television anchorman John Chancellor, the late NBC television correspondent Jessica Savitch, and Casey Casen. The winners were selected by a panel of authorities in the field of voice. The awards were given to increase public sensitivities to good voice quality and to help promote the month of May as Better Hearing and Speech Month. You can add other names to this list, but make an effort to identify and listen to good voices.

As you train yourself to listen for the characteristics that you like in a voice and for the characteristics that you dislike in a voice, you will become better able to judge your own vocal characteristics.

As you go about your daily activities make mental notes about the voices that surround you. As soon as possible, transform those mental notes into written notes. Keep one or two index cards or a small note pad with you at all times. You will find that you can jot notes inconspicuously as you move through your day.

> George talks so loud that I have to step back when I am standing close to him.
>
> Sue has a soft voice, but she articulates every word distinctly. She does not sound stilted. I like to listen to her.
>
> Reverend Jones' voice is much too high pitched for his size and age.
>
> Jim's voice sounds very nasal.

Mary speaks so rapidly that I can hardly follow what she is saying.

During a workshop for training board members of community organizations, one participant was told, "You did an excellent job presenting the material, but you were at a real disadvantage. I had to get accustomed to your voice before I could listen to what you were saying."

The woman in question has a very soft voice that sounds as if it belongs to a much younger person. Her voice does not fit her body or personality.

Many women are faced with this problem. In the past they have been encouraged and rewarded for "girlish" behavior. Now this practice is out-of-step with the demands being placed on women to take active leadership roles in business, church, and community activities. The "little girl" image is no longer appropriate.

Roles and rules in today's society are changing rapidly. Women in leadership roles will find their jobs easier and their potential greater if they train their voices to reflect their total image—body, personality, education, and background.

Much of the potential for voice improvement depends on your becoming a good listener to all types of voices and learning to discriminate those characteristics that appeal to you and those that do not. Once you have selected those characteristics which you like you can work toward achieving them and consciously set out to eliminate those that detract from your effectiveness. You have become knowledgeable about voices and what makes them effective and what causes them to be ineffective.

If you are one of the group of people who has a true voice disorder, you should make an appointment as soon as possible to be evaluated by a speech pathologist. This voice specialist can tell you immediately what steps you need to take to improve your voice. You will find a speech pathologist at a community speech and hearing center, university, hospital, or in private practice. Consult the yellow pages or contact the American Speech-Language and Hearing Association, 10801 Rockville, Pk., Rockville, MD 20852.

10
Speeches of Introduction

What are you going to do? You feel trapped, and there seems to be no escape. You have agreed to introduce the speaker at the annual church banquet, and you can't think of a single thing to say. In fact, you think (as you clutch your throat) that you may never talk again.

First things first. Get a cup of coffee, a sheet of paper, and a pen. It is time to take stock of the situation. What do you know at this moment?

You know the date and time of the banquet. Write that at the top of the paper.

You know the theme of the banquet. Write the theme under the date.

You know the approximate number of people who will be present and that there will be both men and women in attendance. Enter this information.

You know that some very special guests will be present. List their names and functions.

You know the name of the guest speaker. Write the speaker's name under the other information.

You now have before you your raw material. You have the known facts. These can help you plan and can also help keep you from being surprised. If some unexpected situation arises, you will be better able to deal with it.

It is time to go to work. Answer these questions: Who is the speaker? You already know his name, but what are his special qualifications? Make a list. Use a small index card.

Why was the guest speaker invited? Does he have some special connection with your church or denomination? Is he a past president or an officer of a state or national organization? Make a list of these also using a separate index card.

Is she a celebrity whose name is a household word? Is her presence significant? Have you met her before?

National figures, heads of agencies, professors, and professional speakers often have biographical information about themselves already prepared. Usually they will send this to the program chairman in advance upon request.

People who speak infrequently usually do not have such information already prepared, but you can obtain it by calling their office or home. Call the person directly. Explain your purpose and ask only those things you really need to know. Do not chat.

Speeches of Introduction

Your object is to prepare as much in advance as possible. You are doing it in a logical step-by-step approach.

You now have more material than you can use. You see, you are not the featured speaker. You should limit your remarks to no more than three minutes. The President of the United States is introduced very simply: "Ladies and Gentlemen, the President of the United States."

Select the most important and most interesting information about the speaker. Make a new list on another index card. Include that information which will connect him to your congregation. Do not attempt to include everything the speaker has done. Read the list aloud several times. Are you satisfied with the information?

Stand up. Tell me about the speaker. Introduce him to me as if we were meeting at your home for a dinner party. What interests do we share?

Turn on your tape recorder. Time yourself. Be very stingy with the time. Remember, you will probably speak more rapidly on the night of the banquet. You are almost ready.

Decide on your clothing for the evening. Does it need to go to the cleaners? Get everything ready by the weekend before the banquet. If you have young children at home, make plans for them in advance. Every detail taken care of now will give you greater confidence when the time arrives.

When the date comes for the banquet, arrive at least thirty to forty-five minutes early. Meet the speaker if you have not already done so. Check any last-minute details with him. You are well-prepared. The chairperson has confidence in you or she would not have asked you to introduce the speaker. You have done your homework well. Your job now is to focus attention on the speaker. It is time for you to begin.

(This article first appeared as, "Ladies and Gentlemen" in the July, 1979, issue of *Church Training* and is used here with permission of the publisher.)

Appendix

Worksheet A

My Goal—to conquer stage fright
As my first commitment to reach my goal, I will speak to the _____ class on _____ (date). Others to whom I have made this commitment, in addition to myself, are _____ and _____.
Signed_____
Date_____

Worksheet B

For my presentation on _____(date) I will read (Scripture)_____ from the (version) _____.
Who is speaking? _____
Who is being spoken to? _____
What is the speaker's mood? _____
What is the listener's mood? _____
What are the circumstances? _____
Who is present? _____

I could summarize the passage this way:

Worksheet C

Speech Preparation

Speech_____
Audience_____
Date_____
What do I want to happen as a result of this speech? This is the purpose of your speech. Keep this foremost in your thinking as you prepare.

_____
_____
_____
_____
_____

Worksheet D

I. What is my opening statement or topic sentence?

_____
_____

II. 1. What is my most important point?

_____
_____

    a. What does it mean? _____

Appendix

    b. Why is it important? _____

    c. What can I compare it to or contrast it with?
    _____

    d. Do I have an example? _____

2. What is my next most important point? ____
_____
_____

    a. What does it mean? _____

    b. Why is it important? _____

    c. What can I compare it to or contrast it with?
    _____

    d. Do I have an example? _____

3. What is my next most important point?
_____
_____

    a. What does it mean? _____

    b. Why is it important? _____

    c. What can I compare it to or contrast it with?
    _____

d. Do I have an example? _____

III. Conclusion

a. How can I summarize my main points?

b. What do I want to leave with my audience?

Worksheet E

Admired Speakers

My nominations for the ten speakers with the voices I most admire are these. The characteristic that attracts me to this person's voice is listed beside the name.

Name	Characteristic

Appendix

Worksheet F

Listed below are some topics that I would like to present talks about. I commit myself to start collecting information about these topics on the dates specified.

Topics	Date Collection Will Begin On
_____	_____
_____	_____
_____	_____
_____	_____
_____	_____
_____	_____
_____	_____
_____	_____
_____	_____
_____	_____
_____	_____
_____	_____
_____	_____
_____	_____
_____	_____

References

Larry Crisman. "Morass of Messages Threaten to Drown Us in Communications". *Baptist Courier.* July 9, 1981.

"Speeches Hard Work for Woman Astronaut." *Charleston (S.C.) News and Courier.* August 3, 1983.

Christopher Stone. "A Country Girl." *Family Circle.* January 12, 1982.

Eugene White. *Practical Public Speaking.* (New York: The Macmillan Company. 1964.)